BEATRI

My Poetic Reflections On Life

Independence Books
Baltimore

© 2000 by Beatrice Toms.
All rights reserved. No part of this book may be reproduced, stored in a retrieval system, or transmitted in any form or by any means without the prior written permission of the publishers, except by a reviewer who may quote brief passages in a review to be printed in a newspaper, magazine, or journal.

Second printing

Cover design: Richard Markey

ISBN: 1-58851-856-6
PUBLISHED BY INDEPENDENCE BOOKS
www.independencebooks.com
Baltimore

Printed in the United States of America

*Mrs Toms writes
all of her poetry in longhand.
She is grateful to her niece, Barbara Stull,
for transforming handwritten poems
into printed verse.*

*She would also like to thank
Richard Lebherz for his interest, and
the generosity of his time and expertise
in helping to bring this book into print.*

*"And to my family and friends
who have encouraged and humored me,
a little old lady, in this feeble attempt
to express myself,
my eternal gratitude..."*

FORWARD

Ever since 1966, Beatrice Toms has been catering parties and dinners throughout Frederick County and beyond until, in a sense, she has achieved a reputation of almost mythic proportions. There are many party givers in Frederick who would not consider giving a party unless "Mrs. Toms", as she is affectionately known, prepared it. Her delicate rolls, her crab meat casseroles, and desserts are recognized on sight by many Fredericktonians. So, it will certainly come as a great surprise to many of them to discover that Mrs. Toms is also a poetess.

Her poems seem to come out of thin air, many of them already composed and ready for readers to enjoy.

"It all began back in 1998," she explains, "when I had been talking on the telephone to a friend who had been having some difficult problems to face. I can remember coming back out into the kitchen, and I remember clearly picking up a pencil. Then, out of nowhere, words began to spill onto the paper in front of me, and I have been writing poems ever since then."

Beatrice Toms considers her life a journey that she is on, and the poems she writes are like signposts along the way, reminding her and her readers of where she has been and where she is going.

Her very strong belief in God holds both her world and her poetry in place.

In "My Journey" she writes:

"I have been content in whatever situation or place I found myself to be, knowing God was in charge of my life's odyssey."

There is a great simplicity and a homespun touch to her poems that should secure her an audience easily.

Richard Lebherz

TABLE OF CONTENTS

9. Fathers
10. My Journey
12. To My New Baby Girl
14. My Son, My Son
16. When God Speaks To Me
19. Sunrise Sunset
21. The Housewife
22. Prayer of Thanksgiving
23. Little Old Lady
24. To Teachers
25. To My Mother
26. A Man And A Woman
28. My Song
29. A Little Boys Prayer
30. The Bachelor
34. You Hold My Hand
36. The Bore
38. Tragedy
40. Reflections
41. To Farmers
46. From a Mother's Heart
49. Bonnie
50. My Dream
53. What Will I Be
55. What Makes A House A Home
58. The Back Roads
60. Happiness
62. Sail On Sail On
63. When Time Paints Our Portrait
65. Words
67. The Game Of Life
69. Speak To Me My Soul
70. Wedding Vows
71. The Old Stone House
74. Please Be My Friend
75. Light For Tomorrow
76. House Cleaning Time
78. Let Me Live
80. Morning Prayer
81. The Rose
83. Baby Boy Lost
85. God Is
87. Life Can Be Beautiful
89. From My Kitchen Window
92. Tell Someone You Love Them
94. Twilight Love
96. Yesterday
100. He Thought Her Bonny
102. Forever Together
103. Message Of Spring
104. My Vision
106. Lament
109. The Marathon of Life
111. Little One Lost

FATHERS

The dictionary says, "The father is the founder of his race or line or clan,
The one who assumes the responsibility for the care and welfare of his family,"
And from the beginning of time that has been God's plan for man.....

To his son he is the teacher, preacher, and example of all things manly;
and sometimes just to play ball and stuff he comes in mighty handy,
To his daughter, he is her knight in shining armor,
who will let nothing in this world ever harm her;
To his wife, he is husband, partner, and friend,
The one who will love, honor, and cherish her to the end;
To himself, he is provider, mediator, and motivator,
whose concern is for his family first and for himself later,
But to God he is his best hope for a better world,
the bearer of the torch of decency and honor,
that he may pass it on to each son and to each daughter.
Quite a heavy load for any one man to carry,
and there must be times he grows very weary,
Then, may God grant him the strength, the wisdom, and the love,
to fulfill this awesome task ordained from above,
For what better success in life could there be,
Than to raise a descent and honorable family.
So to every father who has answered the call,
May we say, "Thank You Fathers",
and may God bless you one and all,

MY JOURNEY

I have had a long, long journey in this life of mine.
I can only marvel, how quickly has gone by the time.
I have climbed life's highest mountains,
and forged deep treacherous streams.
I have cried my private tears and dreamed my secret dreams.
I have known my share of happiness and deepest sorrow, too.
But through the ups and downs of life, God has seen me through.
I have let my mind take me, to all the wonderful places,
I couldn't go in reality, and I have traveled these
many, many places by land and air and sea.

I have borne my children and watched them grow
into some of the nicest people I'll ever know.
I have lived to see grandchildren, great-grandchildren,
and great-great-grandchildren too , I hope to see.
May God bless them each one, these, my life's legacy.
I have loved, and been loved, and am loved, this I know.
For in so many ways, family and friends let it show.

BEATRICE TOMS

I have been content in whatever situation or place
I found myself to be, knowing God was in charge
of my life's Odyssey.
I always felt I was in the place He wanted me to be,
doing what I was doing, and doing it happily.
For God gave me the strength, the will, and the opportunity.

What more could any one ask of life than I have already been given?
My life's clock has long since struck eleven;
and now I look forward someday to a life of peace and joy,
with friends and loved ones, forever more,
at home, in heaven.

TO MY NEW BABY GIRL

I couldn't have been more happy when you arrived today.
They told me you were a little girl and hurriedly took you away.
When they returned and placed you in my arms my joy was so complete.
Your little face is so beautiful and your tiny body smells so sweet.
Your skin is like satin and you have the right number of fingers and toes.
You are so very perfect with a tiny little button nose.
What will I name you I will really have to ponder, will it be Beth, or Mary, or Jane,
and then my mind begins to wander.
Will you have curly hair, and what will you wear, to your very first day at school.
You will just be so bright and always at the top of your class.
Oh, how rapidly the days go by as into High School you pass.
You are so involved in school activities now I scarcely see you at all.
Then off to college you go to prepare for a great career.
Will you be a doctor, a chemist, a teacher, or maybe you'll be a nurse.

BEATRICE TOMS

You are homecoming queen, your dad and I are so very proud.
You seem to be so happy, as though you are walking on a cloud
and then one day you come to me and say, you've met a nice young man
and sometime soon you plan to be his bride.
You love him so much and want always to be by his side.
As you walk down the aisle, you are a vision in white satin and lace.
I know you must be so happy for there's a lovely smile upon your face.
You've been married now a year and a half and what is that you're telling me
That before very long a grandmother, a grandmother I am going to be!
I am so excited, I wonder what will it be, a boy or a girl, I just can hardly wait.
And then I can feel my heart pounding and with a sudden start I am awake.
I feel you there beside me, and realize this has all just been a dream.
I reach out my hand to touch you, my little baby girl and draw you closer to me.
I kiss your soft little cheek and promptly go back to sleep.

MY SON, MY SON

My son, my son, I hold you in my arms,
for you were just born today.
A most precious gift from God,
the answer to my fervent prayers.
I'll try to be the best Dad in the world.
I'll share your joys and calm your fears
and we'll be a loving father and son
throughout all our coming years.

My son, my son, you're twelve years old
you are my pride and joy, as anyone can see,
and there are those who say you look a lot like me.
I have taught you how to read a book,
to sail a boat, and bait a hook,
to build a campfire, to drive a nail,
and even to plant a tree.
We have shared so many happy times together.
The best of buddies we have come to be.

My son, my son, you're twenty one
a handsome young man with strength and
honor and integrity;
I have tried to teach you right from wrong

and many of the mysteries of life.
Your faith is so strong, and I suspect before long,
you'll be thinking of taking a wife.

My son, my son, I look at you now
and a tear is in my eye;
as you hold your newborn son in that same special way
that I held you, was that only yesterday?
And then you turn to me and say in a voice so very sincere,
Dad dear dad, with God's help I'll try to be
the best dad in the world,
just like the dad you have been to me.

And so it goes generation to generation
from father to son and father to son;
The hopes and dreams, the do's and don'ts
of living a good life.
Of giving and sharing, of loving and caring,
to do your best for your family.
So hope your hopes, and dream your dreams,
and make your years together the best they can be.
Not just for the sake of those you love.
But for all, yes, for all of humanity.

WHEN GOD SPEAKS TO ME

A very happy soul I try to be,
and when there are days, a cloud ore me lays,
I listen very carefully, and in a voice kind and gentle,
God speaks to me.

In nature's sights and sounds his pure love abounds,
and I know He is speaking to me.
In the sound of a mocking bird sitting high in a tree,
singing his heart out and singing just for me.
In the rustle of leaves on some nearby trees,
or the whisper of a soft summer breeze,
God speaks to me.

I watch the flight of wild geese in the spring,
and I watch them in the fall,
playing follow the leader so high in the
sky above us all.
I hear the plaintive call of a lone mourning dove,
and it speaks to me of God's perfect love.
I see a fleecy white cloud in a azure blue sky
slowly drifting by.
Or watch a clear mountain stream flowing
ever downward to the sea.

I hear a soft gentle rain on my window pane,
and I know the grass will be green again,
And God speaks to me

I hear the laughter of happy little children
joyfully running about at play;
like innocence in motion,
and suddenly I am filled with deep emotion.
May all their lives be as happy as they are today,
and please God, bless them each one, I pray.
And God speaks to me.

I see a young mother rocking her little one so that
it doesn't cry,
just rocking and humming a soft sweet lullaby.
A couple of baby kittens playing tag with their mother
in the warm noonday sun,
or an old man just resting when his hard days' work is done.
And God speaks to me.

And what is more beautiful on a cold winters' night,
than a glorious moon and a million stars shining so bright.
The new fallen snow makes a blanket of white,

where ice crystals, like diamonds, dazzle our eyes,
beneath the beautiful starlit skies.
And God speaks to me

It is God's world if only we can see,
and His sounds are all around if we choose to hear.
So I listen and I watch very eagerly,
for I know he is near when His voice I hear,
and I listen very carefully;
when in a whisper kind and gentle,
God speaks to me.

SUNRISE SUNSET

I watched a sunrise this morning
with colors of every known hue.
A beautiful new day was dawning
with so many, many things to do
and I thought to myself how our life
is like a day in time.

As in a day there is a sunrise and a sunset too,
so it is with our lives as we are passing through.
Our hopes, our dreams, our plans, as we begin our life anew.
A beautiful new day dawning, and hopefully, a beautiful sunset too.
It is what we do in between that can make this wonderful hope come true.

Did we lend a helping hand, did we try to understand
another's point of view.
Did we learn to forgive, to live and let live.
Did we try to be honest and true.
Did we learn from life's lessons and count all our blessings.
For you know we've had quite a few.
Did we run our life's race at our best pace
and did we thank God for His mercy and grace?

*Then our sunset can be a beautiful view
for memories are the colors that reflect our days.
Our thoughts, our deeds, and our ways,
if we did our very best and trust a loving God for the rest.
And we are sure His promises are true.
Then sunset, yes, our sunset will be beautiful too.*

THE HOUSEWIFE

She was so tired, today had been so demanding,
so much to do, and so little time.
How could she be so weary?
Had she been too harsh on the children this morning.
The bills, the mortgage, the phone.
How could she hold it all together?
She removed her apron and walked out into the sunshine.
The delicate blue blossoms of the wisteria vine
danced gracefully to the rhythm of
a gentle southern breeze.
She smiled and closed her eyes.

It was spring again, the air was fragrant with
the scent of newly mown hay and the sweet,
sweet smell of blooming lilacs.
Why had she been so blue, so sad, so unhappy?
God was in His heaven, and all was right with the world.
There would be better days ahead.
She slowly walked back into her kitchen and
carefully tied her apron around her slender waist,
as a gentle sense of peace caressed her soul,
and a happy little tune sang within her heart,
and somewhere up there an angel smiled.

PRAYER OF THANKSGIVING

*I lift up my voice, dear Lord, in Thanksgiving and praise
for your constant love, and mercy, and grace.
I thank you for the wondrous gifts you have given to me.
That I may be the kind of soul you would want me to be.
I thank you for the two strong hands, you have given me to use;
that I may work and earn my daily bread;
for my mind, spirit, and body must be fed.
For my two feet, to walk in your way;
and for my mind, that bids me from evil stay.
For my eyes to see the beauty,
that on this earth abounds.
For my ears to hear sweet music and song,
and the laughter of my children;
or their cry for help if something has gone wrong.
A sense of smell, the sweet,
sweet fragrance of flowers to enjoy.
And a spirit of patience, little can annoy.
But most of all, dear Lord in heaven above;
I thank you for the happy heart, you have
placed within my breast,
that I may know the joy, the utter joy,
of giving and receiving love.*

LITTLE OLD LADY

On the street they passed her by,
without a friendly smile.
She was just a little old lady
so infirm, so fragile, so forlorn.

How could they know she had once been like them,
beautiful, young, energetic, and strong.
She too, had laughed, and danced, and sung her song.
And lain in the arms of the man she loved,
and dreamed that beautiful dream.
She had borne his children, and held them
tenderly to her breast.
She had loved, and nurtured, and protected
them from all harm.
But now, her birdlets had flown,
off to their own exciting new worlds,
and she was alone, all alone.
Just a little old lady,
so infirm, so fragile, so forlorn.

TO TEACHERS

Oh, the power, you have in your hand,
to help a child's mind to understand.
To make each day a new adventure,
be it in math, or science, or music, or art.
The child reaches out for the knowledge you impart.

So consider it a challenge and a great opportunity,
which also carries with it serious responsibility.
To show each child how exciting knowledge can be _ _ _.
To encourage that child to become the best he can,
be it teacher, preacher, doctor or successful business man.
You will have had a very large part in what he becomes ultimately.

So count each child as part of your life's success.
That you may look back on those years with pride,
and know you were always there with help to provide.
Many of us recall special teachers who would
always encourage and challenge us to learn all we could,
for they opened the door to learning and knowledge,
whether it was in elementary, high school, or college.

We still remember those teachers and revere their name,
for without them, our lives would never have been the same.
So count your teaching career an opportunity grand,
for, oh the power, the awesome power, you hold in your hand!

TO MY MOTHER

Oh, mother dear, I hope you can hear
the song I sing to you.
I want you to know I love you so
and hope that you love me, too.

Oh mother dear I hope you can hear
the song I sing to you.
You gave me life, then sent me away
I just don't understand.
Did I make you sad or was I bad
I really need to know.

Oh mother dear, I hope you can hear
The song I sing to you.
I never knew your gentle touch or even a tender kiss.
I only know I miss you so,
and hope you miss me too.

Oh mother dear I hope you can hear
the song I sing to you.
I want you to know I love you so
and hope that you love me, too.

A MAN AND A WOMAN

I saw them walking together one day,
Holding each other's hand.
It was a beautiful sight to see.
Their love seemed so strong
Like a beautiful song, where the melody lingers on.

When a man loves a woman and a woman loves a man,
it must be one of the sweet mysteries of life.
How does it show, and how do we know, if their devotion is true?
He may be rich or he may be poor with only the
bare necessities of life.
If love is mature, she feels so secure, just in being his wife.

Things do not always happiness bring;
and she is content just to be wearing his ring.
Just to be where he is, is all she really needs.
And on his constant love her very soul feeds.
She will stay by his side and her love will abide;
if their days are all fair, or if there be stormy weather;
they will see it through, and they will see it through together.

She is his oasis in the vast dry sands of life;
where he comes at the end of each long tiring day;
for a cold, refreshing drink of encouragement,
understanding, and love.

And he is her rock, her port in the storm
always there to reassure her, and kiss
away all her fears.
She will always be his beautiful bride no matter
how quickly go by the years;
and he will forever be the man who stood beside her
and promised to share her laughter and tears.

Loving and caring, each thinking first of the other.
In good times and bad, heart to heart, and hand in hand;
just living the best life they can.
And that's how it shows, and that's how we know,
when a man loves a woman, and a woman
loves her man.

MY SONG

I sing because I am happy.
I am happy because God loves me.
God loves me because I am His child.
I am His child because he made me.
God made me to worship him.
I worship him because he is my Father.
Because he is my Father I sing,
and this is my song.
I sing because I am happy

A LITTLE BOY'S PRAYER

Hello God this is me, Jimmy, again.
I just wanted to tell you what a good time I had today,
Missie and Bobbie came over to my house to play.
We played hide and seek and I got caught twice.
I like to play with Missie and Bobbie they are both so nice.
We always have such a good time.
And oh while we were playing I found a dime.
And God please bless Mommy and Daddy,
and my little sister Mary, she is too little to play you know.
And please bless all the rest of the people in the world
And specially my little puppy Rusty, I love him so.
Hope you had a nice day too.
Good night for now, I love You.

THE BACHELOR

His mother had spoken to him this morning,
on a subject quite familiar.
He was forty years old and never had taken a bride.
He was getting older each day she said,
and needed a good wife by his side.

He had dated so many, yet had never found any;
who quite lived up to his expectations.
They were either too young or too old.
Some were too timid, some were too bold.
Some had faces too plain and others seemed
not to have a brain.
He thought of himself as being quite a catch,
with money and looks and a wonderful personality.
He had to find someone who would be a perfect match.

That night he went to a charity ball.
To simply pass away the time,
and there he saw her, across the ballroom floor.
So fair of face, a vision in satin and lace.
A body just about perfect, a lady with charm and grace.

Slowly he approached her and asked
her if she cared to dance.
Somewhat shyly she accepted his hand
and they moved into the dance, to the music of the band.
As they waltzed across the room,
her feet scarcely touched the floor.
She was so graceful, so utterly charming
that indeed he found her most disarming.

Another dance or two and lots of conversation too,
she almost always agreed and
seemed to hang on his every word;
as though his brilliant ideas she before had never heard.

She looked into his eyes and said
she thought him to be very wise.
Her admiration for him she didn't try to disguise.
When she touched his cheek he found it hard to speak.
Why did he find her so absolutely charming?
Was he getting sentimental, he found that quite alarming.

*So he asked if he could take her home
and she seemed so quickly to agree.
When they reached her door, he thanked
her for the lovely evening.
But really he would have to leave
and simply couldn't stay,
as he had a very, very important appointment
very early the next day,
and that he would call her soon, maybe next Monday.*

*The next morning his mother asked him
about the ball as mothers sometimes do.
And he told her about the lovely lady
and all that had happened, too.
His mother began to hope for a happy ending,
and with the lovely lady more time he would be spending.
And then he said in a voice quite rational;
"though I found her most attractive,
I won't be seeing her anymore.*

There's no way any one person could be so perfect,
and though I found her most distracting,
I can't believe she was really, really, real;
so I must conclude she was only acting."

So once a bachelor always a bachelor, they say.
They dream their dreams about the perfect mate,
and if they don't find one, they blame it all on fate.
Once in a while they wish they had a second chance,
but sad to state, by that time, it's almost always too late.

YOU HOLD MY HAND

Dear Father in heaven above, as I look back on
my long and sometimes arduous life,
I marvel at the many times,
life could have been over for me;
had You not been there to hold my hand.
My early life was fraught with many changes;
that as a child were so hard to understand.
But You were always there to comfort me,
and hold my hand.
If I sometimes stumbled and fell,
You were there to pick me up.
To give me courage to take the next step,
and to move on.

Through grave illness You were there, holding
my hand and bidding me to be strong.
Through accidents and deep despair,
with the touch of Your hand,
once again I felt secure.

Through grief and mourning You were there,
giving me comfort and strength to endure.
You have been a balm unto my very soul
a never ending source of strength and hope.

From the time I was a little child,
until now when I am old.
And when my time on earth is ore,
and on my life You close the door.
I will step through the portals,
into Your garden of peace and rest.
And I know You'll be there
to hold my hand forever more.

THE BORE

This is a tale of a man misunderstood.
It happened at a fund raiser in our little town.
The event in support of a local politician of some renown.
And there's a lesson here to be learned,
a lesson for our own good !
Don't judge another, for we, too, could be misunderstood.

All the right people were there, definitely the upper crust.
There were doctors and lawyers and bankers and such.
And others quite political.
I saw two ladies conversing in an attitude most confidential.
As a certain gentleman approached,
I heard one lady say to the other in a tone very critical.
Avoid him if you can, he's such a boring man,
not very clever, so quiet, so little to say.

The man sensing their rebuff, turned away.
A moment late he followed a waiter into the kitchen
And said, " I'd like to use the phone if I may.
Hello, son, this is daddy, I am sorry I had
to be so cross with you this morning;

but the little lie you told me, gave me much concern
and there are lessons in life we have to learn.
For if a respected grown man you hope to be,
you have to grow up with truth and honor and integrity.
We have to be honest and respect ourselves you see.
I'll be home soon, Daddy loves you. "

It occurred to me then, so much the ladies could have learned
from this man they had so coldly spurned.
About life and it's meaning, of loving and caring
about those we love.
For this was his first priority.
And it was plain to see, he was not in the majority.
Though a bore they had perceived him to be,
and just a dull, uninteresting man was all they could see;
What a revelation there could have been;
Had they taken the time to know the good,
good man within.

TRAGEDY

*He lay on the street, the victim of a single
bullet from an opposing gang.
They said he was just fourteen years old;
yet there he lay, still, lifeless, and cold.*

*On a cold December morn he had been found
on a doorstep in the city.
Wrapped in a single blanket,
and just two days old.
His parents were unknown,
or so I've been told.*

*Moved from shelter to shelter,
and home to home.
No one to love him, no one to hold him,
no one to show him they cared.
Most of his days were spent,
just being so lonely, and oh, so scared.
Finally the street had reclaimed him.
He had tried to make it in the city,
the city so big, so harsh, so cold.*

His gang had called him Flukie,
he just didn't seem to have the degree of
anger and violence to survive in this
hostile, friendless place.
And now he had been cut down and
was no more, no more.

So sad the story, not just that he had died,
but that he had never been able to live.
There was no one to claim him,
no one to mourn him,
no one to remember his name.
Tragedy, tragedy, oh tragedy.
Only God can count the cost
a child, a mind, a soul,
Lost, lost, lost.

REFLECTIONS

Courage, with so many, many faces,
we see it in high and low places.
In crisis, it's doing what really needs to be done:
when our first instinct is to turn around and run.

Truth is forever a friend.
From our youth to our life's end.
We need never amend any statement we've made:
if always with the truth we have stayed.

Try never to hurt another human being deeply,
if you apologize sincerely, the pain may go away:
but the scar will remain with them
until their dying day.

Imagination is parent to action
if we can imagine it or dream it;
we can do almost anything,
at least to our own satisfaction.

We choose in life the paths we will take;
be it the high or the low roads;
and at the end it will be easy to see
which of life's roads we chose.

TO FARMERS

I wish I could dedicate a plaque ,
or write a song of praise, to the farmers of this land.
For I marvel at their character, and dedication,
and they're always there to lend one another a helping hand.
First of all a good farmer has to love the land and the work he is doing;
and be happy and content with the demanding life he is pursuing.

He needs to have veterinary skills, to care for his animals;
any hour of the night or day.
For many times they must be treated immediately and without delay.
Sometimes he has to be a mechanic,
and be able to repair any piece of machinery;
to get each nut and bolt back in the right place,
and often against time and darkness it becomes quite a race.
For many times the break occurs out in the field,
and the repair just has to be done,
so that sowing, or mowing, or reaping can go on.

He has to be a herdsman to determine the health,
feeding, and production of his herd.
Often decisions are made, after he has poured over
periodicals, and farm magazines,
or with other dairymen he has conferred.

*He had better be an accountant to determine
his production, his losses or gains;
and his financial status year to year;
in order to keep his farm operation in just the right gear.*

*He has to be an optimist, to have courage to
plant again, when this year's crops have fallen
far below his expectation.
Then he must think positively on things
that give him real motivation.*

*He has to be an economist to know when, where,
or why, to buy or sell; be it cattle, machinery, or crops;
and to know when the market is up and to know when the market drops.*

*He has to be a realist to accept whatever time
or fate hands him, and decide where to go from there;
and he has to be a man, who when things
get really rough; can handle most any disappointment
or hardship, because he's made of the right stuff.
His work is never done, no matter how
many hours he stays in the sun.
He is in the field before sunup and often
long after sundown, trying to get it all done.*

He plants and harvests to feed his cows, that
give the milk, that makes the butter and cheese,
and many other things I could name.
And the cows reproduce their own kind, to
start the production cycle over again.

He practices good husbandry on the land
and the soil that he loves.
Restoring vital nutrients back into the ground;
that have been eroded by crops, wind, and rain,
and religiously, year after year, he returns
those precious elements back into the land again.

He takes pride in his crops and wants them to be
an expression of his stewardship and care.
And there is no more beautiful sight to see, than a field
of new mown hay, stretched out as far as the eye can see;
in perfect windrows waiting to be baled.
Or acres and acres of golden grain swaying in a gentle breeze.
And row after row of black green corn that
seems to be reaching upward to the sky; with heavy ears that
give promise of an excellent crop, by and by.

He prays for rain in the time of drought and
gives prayers of thanks to God for his blessing;
when the rain comes pouring down on his thirsty fields;
for he knows good intermittent showers will greatly increase his yields.
God is his partner, or should we say he is God's partner,
for the farmer plants the fields and God gives
the increase, that all of mankind may be fed;
with milk, and meat, vegetables and grain,
and other products to numerous to name;
that man, his health and well being can maintain.

The farmer still holds on to some of the old axioms
that have been handed down through the years;
from his great-grandfather to his grandfather, to
his father, who passed them on to him.
"Don't plow when it's too wet, or a very hardened soil you surely will get."
Plant this crop or that crop before a certain date;
for if you don't, it'll just be too late.
Plant certain crops in the up or the down sign from the Old Farmers
Almanac, or for nothing, you'll be breaking your back.

And if it doesn't rain on St Swithin's Day, on
July fifteen, you're in for a forty day dry spell, with little or no rain in between.
And a man's word is his bond, and just a warm
firm handshake, can seal almost any deal.

His ever faithful wife and loyal sons are always by his side,
with strength, encouragement and assistance to provide.
For that's the only way the family farm can ever survive.

So hats off to the farmers all over this land,
for they are a very special breed,
and we all know they have the awesome task
of millions upon millions of people to feed.
So we pray, may God grant them, each one,
the strength, the courage, the faith, and the stamina they will need;
and let us all hope, that in this enormous task and challenge;
they will continue to succeed; in supplying enough food,
for the hosts of people they will have to feed.

FROM A MOTHER'S HEART

Today is Mother's Day, on which we honor mothers all over the world.
And we are here to honor mothers in our own family.
Gloria, Joan, Deborah, Diane, and me.

But today I would like to honor and thank each one of you, my children;
For the respect and love you have given to me.
And for the pride you have made me feel over the years,
as you continue to bless me.

You have been my purpose in life and
you have exceeded the hopes
and dreams I have had for each of you.
For you have always tried to do, a little more
than you were asked to do.

You have blessed me with grandchildren, and
great-grandchildren, too, of which I am very proud.
Each one is so very special in his or her own unique way.
And they warm their mother's
heart each and every day.

To you young mothers I would like to say,
the bond between a mother and her child
is endless and eternal;
for there is no more undying love,
than that which is maternal.

I can only wish for you young mothers
the same sense of accomplishment and pride
that you have given and continue to give to me.
For, you, my children, have made me the
proud and happy mother you see.

A mother's children are her life's work,
her highest goal, her first priority to raise
happy, healthy, well adjusted children;
and from this work of love she will never shirk.

I, salute you, my children, Joan, Patty, and Donnie
for being the kind of individuals you have become,
children any mother could be proud of.

And though you are different one from the other;
In many ways you are the same, for you all have
the same mother.

One generation follows the other
in steady succession;
And each generation will be remembered
for it's own dedication.

I pray God may watch over and be
with you through the years;
that you, too may know the same sense of joy,
and accomplishment and pride you
have given and continue to give to me.

And this last thought I leave with you
before we part;
I want you to know I love you so much;
and I thank you from the bottom of a
proud, happy, and grateful Mother's heart.

BONNIE

Her name was Bonnie, a beautiful sensitive Dalmatian.
She was always active, always on the go, always curious.
She seemed to approach life in a manner most serious.
One day I watched her feverishly digging in my flower bed,
in a frenzy, throwing the rich black soil over - her - head.
She seemed to be so sure there had to be a bone down there somewhere
And this activity had become quite a habit with her.
If she met with no success; she would stop, catch her breath,
and shake herself off, and look around for another likely sight;
then she would dash off and begin digging again with all her might.
I smiled and thought, how like Bonnie I was,
always digging in search of some goal, some cause, I had in mind.

Like Bonnie, I would approach each challenge,
each goal, with the same fervor,
the same enthusiasm, the same zeal.
There were times I would succeed and there
were times I would fail.
I was not always sure if I was digging in or digging out.
As I look back now, I realize the joy,
the real joy, had been in the digging.
So whether I won, or whether I lost
I never really counted the cost,
for always there had been the hope I would succeed,
and , after all, both Bonnie and I had our puppies to feed.

MY DREAM

I dreamed a dream, such a beautiful dream it filled my heart with joy.
All the world was at peace; and happiness was everywhere.
Wonder of wonders; how could this possibly be,
and then I looked around me and I could see ——
Parents were devoted to their children and took time
to listen to their every concern;
and children respected their parents and from their wisdom,
seemed eager to learn.

Everyone was willing to work for their living;
and never grumbled or complained that life was unfair.
People said please and thank you and to their
old folks gave the greatest of love and care.
Everyone you met was courteous and treated you as a friend;
and if they owned something you needed to borrow,
they were more than willing to lend.

There were no barred windows or locks on the doors.
Each person respected the other's property and privacy,
and they respected yours.
There was no one to fear, no angry words were ever said;
and everyone felt safe and secure in his or her own bed.

*There were no more wars and international problems
were solved with a hand shake and a promise,
that was kept to the very letter of the word;
and if anyone suggested that could be risky they
would have thought such a suggestion absurd.*

*Guns were unnecessary for violence was nil;
and everyone could drink of life's blessings
until they had their fill.
There was no jealousy, or envy, or strife,
and everyone was living a happy contented life.*

*I awoke and looked around me and what a difference I could see;
Tears filled my eyes and a great sadness came over me.
There was greed, and malice, and anger all around,
and where was the Eutopia that only a dream ago,
I had found?*

*Our Lord gave us such a beautiful world for the
nurture and enjoyment of man;
but, oh, how very far we have drifted from His plan.
We are His children and He loves us all equally;*

*and He wants us to be happy and live
together in peace and harmony.
God is watching us, and how sad He must be,
to see how we treat one another and that all
around Him, His frustrated, unhappy children
is all He can see.*

*Why can't we do better, at least we should really try.
If only in our own little world around us,
with family and neighbors and those who are passing by.
This we know to be true; it can't all be changed in a day;
but each little act of kindness, or forbearance, or forgiveness,
can start us going the right way.
A smile, a handshake, or a friendly word or two.
We are not alone in this world and what we do affects others;
And what they do, affects us, too.
We cannot be angry with others, and at the same time,
with ourselves be happy too.
It all has to start somewhere; so let it begin with me and you.
It was just a dream, but such a beautiful dream and,
we know, sometimes dreams really can come true.*

WHAT WILL I BE

They sat on the river bank, fishing pole in hand;
exchanging father-son small talk, man to man.
"What should I try to do in my life and what would
you like me to be," the son asked.
The father was silent for a few moments as though
he was thinking it through, then he turned to his son and said,
"I want you to do in your life what you really want to do.
There are so many careers you could choose,
you could become a banker, politician, or teacher,
farmer, electrician or mechanic, or preacher It's really up to you.
But whatever you choose, be the very best you can be,
and never settle for mediocrity.
We become in life the person we really want to be,
and if we set some definite goal we must work
toward it with mind, body, and soul.

God gives us choices of the life we would like to pursue.
He gives us talents and aptitudes for many careers we alone can choose.
If we ask for His guidance, very few wrong decisions will we make.
He gives us direction, but we choose the path we will take.
He opens many different doors for us, if only we would knock.

*But when our ship of life sets sail we sometimes remain
standing on the dock, afraid to take a chance, afraid some
new field to explore, life is what we make it, it can be good, and even more.
If we learn to broaden our visions, many great opportunities may arise.
We can remain standing on the low ground or reach upwards to the skies.
We must steer our course carefully, through many a rough sea and shoal,
it is only by perseverance and dedication we can reach our ultimate goal.
But when we find the niche made for us, we will know it immediately;
and we will find our life's work rewarding and giving us a sense of dignity.
If we love what we are doing and give attention to every detail;
we will be successful and rarely, if ever, fail.*

*Life takes a while to examine ourselves and know
who we are, and what we want to achieve.
Don't settle for second best unless that's where you want to be.
Keep striving for your dream, for you alone hold the magic key.
And remember it isn't whether you are rich and famous,
success and happiness, is finding that place in life,
exactly where you want to be.*

BEATRICE TOMS

WHAT MAKES A HOUSE A HOME

What makes a house a home, it's such a subtle thing.
It may be a mansion or a cottage small.
If warmth and love is there, nothing else really matters after all.
When a caring family lives there, it becomes a very special place,
with mutual respect, harmony, and devotion;
held together with bonds of love as strong as steel.
And the care and concern for one another, each one can feel.

Everyone rises early, a good healthful breakfast to share.
Then off to school, the office, or shop for most of the day;
each one receives a hug or pat on the shoulder as they go on their way;
and they look forward to sharing their problems,
or triumphs when they return home at the end of the day.

The aroma of a good home cooked meal permeates the air,
and everyone sits down, Mama's good food to share.
Daddy says grace, all heads are bowed, as he offers
thanks to Providence for His blessings and care.
Supper over and dishes all washed and put away,
Mama picks up her mending, the children do their homework,
and Dad reviews the mail, and the bills that are due to pay.

*Then the children are off to bed where prayers are said
upon their knees, by the side of the bed.
There are good night kisses, enough to go around.
Each child is carefully tucked in;
and contented little sighs are the only sound.*

*Mama plans tomorrow's breakfast, nourishing and tasty,
as are all her menus, and Daddy catches up with the daily news.
Then lights out, for tomorrow is another busy day.
Got to get up early, Dad has another important job to survey.*

*If this all sounds like it happened a long time ago,
perhaps this is true, but maybe we could all
try to do it that way again;
for life did seem to be much happier back then;
family members seemed to know they were loved
and each one cared for the others and
loved the home they shared.
Home was a safe haven, with Mother and Father
always there to comfort and soothe;
and warmth and affection, could heal most any wound.
Home was a magic word, where life's*

little problems could all be solved,
and family was the center, around which our lives revolved.

No matter how far away from home we wander,
the memories remain;
and we long to go back home again.
We all remember the love, the happiness,
the simple pleasures, the fun we shared back then;
and we would give most anything on earth,
if we could do it all over again.

More than anything else we need a sense of belonging,
and being loved unconditionally;
this we had, and more, because we were a family.
How wonderful it would be to return to that
place and time we called home;
with Mother and Father, and sisters and brothers,
all there, just like it used to be.
And from that very special place we would
never again want to roam,
and that's what makes a house, your house and mine,
the place, that hallowed place, we call home.

THE BACK ROADS

The back roads, the beautiful back roads,
it's like being in another world.
The big bustling city, with its noise, clamor,
and congestion I have long since left behind.
I drive through the countryside, then, on to the back roads;
where peace and quiet, I hope I will find.

So quiet, so peaceful, so restful and so stimulating
and fresh is the air; and on the road, yellow butterflies
frolic in the warm summer sun.
Such a beautiful scene, has now become very rare.
I cross cool little streams with their quaint little bridges.
There are many, many, curves in the road and
lots of small bumps and ridges.
The only sound I hear, is the sound of the birds
as they scatter when I pass by, and every now and
then the bright summer sun filters through the trees,
and I can see the clear blue sky.

I pass neat little houses and a small
log cabin every now and then.
There's a couple of cattle and a few
chickens, too, in a small green
pasture, just around the bend.

*I see a little old lady weeding her garden
or maybe she's gathering vegetables for a meal later on.
Her homemade bonnet carefully tied beneath her chin,
to protect her from the sun and the warm summer wind.
Her snowwhite wash is drying on the line,
gaily dancing, to and fro, in the bright sunshine.*

*Her house is surrounded with flowers of many
different kinds; and her white-washed board
fence is covered with pink rambler roses and vines.
There's an old, old man rocking on his front porch
and he raises his hand to say Hi.
I guess on this road he sees very few passersby.*

*I hope you, too, may have the opportunity to have
this same wonderful experience, my friend,
for it's like a trip back in time.
If you do, please drive slowly, so your
soul can take it all in, and I hope you'll
do it real soon, for if you wait too long it
may be all gone by then.*

HAPPINESS

Happiness is such a simple word,
yet so very hard to define.
We are all so very different;
from diverse backgrounds,
places, and times.

Happiness, let's look at the word more closely,
and perhaps we can see, what the word
means to you, and what the word means to me.

To some, seeing nature in all its' beauty.
To others, just living a good life and doing their duty.
To some, it may mean a big expensive car.
To others, just sitting with good buddies at the local bar.
To some, a loving, caring spouse.
To others, a beautiful brand new house.
To some, receiving a very prestigious prize.
To others, seeing the love in another's eyes.

To some, just lots and lots of money.
To others, a very, very special honey.
To some, a couple of wonderful kids.
To others, doing the things that God forbids.
To some, it's always being a winner.
To others, just a good old fashioned, home-cooked dinner.
To some, exploring the woods or sailing the seven seas.
To others, a quiet chat with God upon their knees.

We pick and we choose, sometimes we win,
sometimes we lose, and yet it is always
there for everyone, right before our eyes;
For I have come to find, happiness, true happiness,
is really in our hearts and in our minds.

SAIL ON SAIL ON

Sail on, sail on, oh ship of state,
we are your passengers and crew.
Fly high your colors, the old red, white, and blue.
We will forever be loyal to you.

Emblazoned on your mast head our motto,
"In God We Trust".
Written in the blood of our Valiants,
who sacrificed their lives for us.

With God as our captain and navigator too;
though stormy seas may pound us,
and demons of the deep confound us;
We'll keep right on sailing through.
If ominous clouds should cause us alarm;
we pray our Captain will protect us from harm.

So hoist high your sail, full into the gale,
we cannot, we must not fail.
We have came a long arduous journey,
but with God as our Captain, we still
have a lot more sailing to do.
So sail on, sail on, sail on;
we will forever be loyal to you.

BEATRICE TOMS

WHEN TIME PAINTS OUR PORTRAIT

Have you ever wondered what you will look like when
You grow older; and if you will age gracefully?
I guess the right answer for that would just have to be _____.

Father Time paints our portrait, as sure, as sure can be.
There's no need to order it done, and there is never, ever a fee.
Each day, the thoughts we think, the words we say
And the things we do etch their mark on our personality;
And Father Time keeps right on painting inexorably.

When our portrait is finished, will the eyes be gentle and kind;
Or will they be cold, lifeless and dull, as dull, as dull can be,
Having no sparkle at all.
For the eyes are the windows of the soul, they say,
That reflect our joy and approach to life, day by day.
Will the mouth have a quiet smile, or will there be no smile at all;
With the corners turned down and on the brow a deep dark frown.

My Poetic Reflections on Life

As we grow older, lines are bound to appear,
Will they be lines from smiles and laughter;
Or will they be lines from anger, envy or fear.
Day by day, our likeness is being drawn,
As time paints our portrait for everyone to see.
We can only hope we will be happy and content, you and me.
When time has finished the portrait of the person we have come to be.

WORDS

*Words, ah, words are our means of communication, with
which we express our thoughts, our needs, our desires.
Sometimes they are used in excess, at other times
not at all, when we should an apology express.
They can be inquisitive, humorous, lighthearted or serious.
For they express the full gamut, of the human experience*

*Words can be consoling or they can become controlling.
They can give us courage, or fill us with fear.
They can give us joy and laughter, or bring on many a tear.
There are times they can be encouraging and motivating,
at other times discouraging and devastating.
With loved ones and family, they can bring them
together or tear them apart.
And they have the power to lift a soul or break a heart.*

*The right words can keep the world at peace,
or the wrong words can propel us into war.
It is much more prudent to solve the world's
problems with words, rather than guns, by far.
May we use words to comfort and never to abuse,
or in a heated showdown, be the match that lights the fuse.*

Lord, bridle our tongue before the damage is done,
and help us to think before we speak;
and never, ever use them when our anger is at its peak.
Let our words always be truthful and leave no one deceived;
for words, once spoken can never be retrieved.
Much as the phrase, " we are what we eat", just as valid
is the truism," we are what we speak".

THE GAME OF LIFE

When you come into this world you enter into the game of life.
You will experience the sweet taste of victory, and
the bitter pill of failure and strife.
If you are batting one hundred in a situation only a thousand will do;
step up to the plate and bat in a home run or two.

If life throws you a curve, you just can't handle,
treat it as a learning experience and you'll know what to do,
the next time that old curve comes flying at you,
just muster your nerve and step right up and show them what you can do.
Keep swinging that bat and sooner or later you'll send
that old ball a mile or two.

Once in a while, life may grant you a walk,
but you still have to run the bases before it counts.
If you strike out, don't forget there will be other innings;
although the pressure on you mounts.
Then there are times you may be booed, by those who
think they know more about the game then you do.
The umpires are always there, watching your every move,
to tell you when you are off base and when you are in the groove.

My Poetic Reflections on Life

Your Coach, above all, is counting on you,
He knows your talents and wants to be proud of you,
and if you don't play the game the way He has coached you to,
occasionally, He might just give you a nudge or two.
The game of life just has to be played and there is never an off season;
and you never, ever retire for any reason.

If you have given your best, to which your life's record will attest;
and you are in the final inning of the game you
have played from the very beginning.
You are on third base and headed for home and
you hear the call, safe, safe at home .
What joy there will be when you are called on by name,
to enter into, what we will call;
The Celestial Hall of Fame.

SPEAK TO ME MY SOUL

Speak to me my soul, lead me by your hand,
let my heart rejoice; if that is in your plan.
Keep my mind and being, within God's precious will.
Let me not complain of life's capricious ways.
We are here on earth, for just a few short days.
Help me then to see the joy in all of life, I pray;
that I may help another soul, along life's rugged way.

WEDDING VOWS

As we stand together you and I,
You give me your hand, and I give you mine.
Your heart is my heart, and my heart is yours.
You'll share your life with me,
And I'll share my life with you.
For as long as we live, to each other we will give,
A love that is constant, forever, and true.
This is your pledge to me,
And my eternal pledge to you.

THE OLD STONE HOUSE

*The old house was made of stone, austere
and plain as plain could be.
It was going to be our new home,
having just purchased the farm,
my husband and me.
We were moving from another house,
which by any standard, could be
considered almost grand;
compared to this old stone house we had
bought with the land.*

*A tear slowly coursed down my cheek,
as I looked around me, at this old house so bleak.
There was no central heating, an old wood stove
in the kitchen, and a primitive country sink.
How could I possibly make this a comfortable home,
was all I was able to think.*

*The cold empty rooms were so forbidding,
and the stairs so badly worn,*

*where thousands of footprints had worn them away
as generations had trod them day after day.
I reached down and touched those
old worn stairs, almost reverently;
and this old house, for me, began to take
on a new different identity.*

*Here young men had brought their brides
and began their families;
and tired old folks had sat on the
front porch and watched
their grandchildren at play.
Families had sat around the kitchen table
and exchanged the happenings of the day;
and little ones had climbed these very stairs each night,
and knelt by their beds to pray.*

*I could almost hear the sounds of joy and laughter
that resounded from these walls;
and hear the patter of little feet as they frolicked
up and down the halls.*

Babies had been born here and lived their
entire lives in this place;
and how many souls before me had
occupied this very same space.
And I began to wonder, if some day, would there
be those who would remember my family
and me, when we had become
a part of this old house's history.

As the days and years went by, I began to see, how
blessed I had been to have lived in this old house
with it's many memories,
of those who had lived here through the years
with their families.
For this house, this old stone house had become home,
my home, sweet home to me.

PLEASE BE MY FRIEND

Oh, bid me not, your lover to be,
For I am so afraid.
Your face is so fair and you have such an air,
You take my breath away.
When you look at me and I look at you,
You seem so very sincere.
But what would I do if you were untrue?
My heart would surely break.
You see, I've been down this road before,
And it came to a tragic dead end.
So just for now and if you don't mind,
I'd rather just be your friend.

LIGHT FOR TOMORROW

If we would light tomorrow with today...
Let our thoughts be pure.
Let our hands be sure.
Let our words be true
Let our instincts be kind.
Let our priorities be defined.
Let our anger be subdued.
Let our friendships be renewed.
Then our hearts and spirits,
Will surely be much lighter;
And tomorrow, the world will seem
to be, so much brighter.

HOUSE CLEANING TIME

I chanced to visit my attic one day, to be certain
The windows were made secure.
For a sudden summer storm was on its' way.
While there, I looked around me, almost in dismay.
Things I had long since forgotten, were now covered with dust.
Where I had so carefully stored them away,
That I might possibly use them some other day.
And I promised myself, someday soon I would sort it all out.
I would keep only the useful and good, and discard
The rest of the clutter, as I knew I should.

So it is with our mortal house in which we really live.
The attic of this house, is our mind, where so many, many
Thoughts are carefully tucked away.
We need to concentrate on the beautiful things in life,
And the malefic clutter in our minds, cast away.
The anger, the jealousies, the animosities from some other day.
Imagined affronts that have made us bitter inside,
That we plan to pay back in full someday, whatever may betide.
Do they still continue to upset us, even yet.
Or have we matured enough to forgive and forget.
If we can just give them a toss, nothing of value will be lost.
They only take up space, that could better be used
For a sense of God's mercy and grace.

In the hidden closet of our heart, bulging with broken
Dreams and disappointments that lived and died so long ago,
About which only we and our Maker really know.
Let's bring them out into the light and look them over.
Would they still be appropriate in this place and time.
Or have they been replaced by something much better,
We want to cherish and hold on to, for all time.

In the basement, the deep, deep basement of our soul
When we look down deep inside, is there something there
We have long hidden away that no one else would ever know,
How we cherished and paid it homage untold, day by day.
This deep dark secret down in our soul.
Let's drag it out and replace it with a sense of release
And the sure knowledge of forgiveness.
When with God and man we have made our peace.

House cleaning is most often done in the spring, but if we don't get around to it then;
Before we are aware, fall is here, and the cold frost of reality is in the air.
We need to get our house in order and for the coming days to prepare.
That in the winter of life we may find peace and blessings untold.
When our mortal house, in which we really live, has been cleansed and
refreshed, and we are renewed in our mind, in our heart and in our soul.

LET ME LIVE

Let me live till I die
Let me still dream, let me still try.
Let me still plan, let me do what I can.
Let me still laugh, let me join in the fun.
Let me feel some good thing I have accomplished,
When each long day is done.

Fetter me not with your many concerns,
For the yearning to do what I can , in my heart still burns.
Life is meant to be lived from the beginning to the very end.
Make the most of each day; we don't know what
May be just around the bend.

Place me not in an old rocking chair and tell me I must sit.
And from doing this or that, say I just must quit.
Give me not a music box, to play for me taps,
Rather give me some little chore to do, that I
Let not time unproductive lapse.

Let me rock your babies, I'll be as careful as I can.
Babies having grandmas is part of God's master plan.
Let me give a word of cheer to someone who is sad,

To help them remember happier times they have had.
Let me plant in the fall and look forward to spring,
When time and nature, lovely blossoms will bring.
Let me plant in the spring and look forward with hope
Of the harvest to come in the fall,
When God with His bounty, blesses us all.

There are so many, many things I still want to do;
for living is doing, and doing is living. I know no other way.
Humor me then, please humor me, if you will;
Let me know the joy of endeavor for that is my bent,
So let me do what I can, and that will help me be content.

Oh, my feet are not as nimble, and my
Hands are not as strong as they once were,
But my heart is still young and my mind is still clear,
And blessing upon blessing, I can see the faces of my
Loved ones and their voices I still can hear.
Life can be so rich, life can be so full, as the years go swiftly by.
So, please God, let me live, really live, until the day that I die.

MORNING PRAYER

Awake, awake, oh, beautiful morning,
When first light of day is dawning.
A day of hope and promise too;
Lord help me then thy will to do.
I turn to you in heaven above,
To seek your guidance and abiding love.
Let me now, before you kneel,
The touch of your healing hand to feel.
Keep me then, ever close to thee;
The light of your holy continence to see.
Morning, morning, oh, beautiful morning,
When you are, here to share it with me.

THE ROSE

Most of the other mourners had drifted away as he approached
And knelt to lay, a single rose upon the grave.
Unshaven, with clothes so unkept and in his every movement so very inept.
His head was bowed and his body shook, as his tears flowed
Down on the silent mound; they had so quickly covered with the cold, cold ground.

Who could this young man be, and why was he here and so
Consumed with his grief; as though from his sorrow
And remorse, he could find no relief.
Finally he arose and slowly walked away, but he looked
Back several times, as if he really had wanted to stay.

Each week he returned and knelt by the grave, and strange to see,
The single rose was as fresh as the day he had lain it there.
All the other flowers had faded and been taken away;
But the rose somehow seemed to have taken root,
And grew more beautiful each day.

With each visit he seemed to be more and more at peace with himself.
As though something beautiful down deep in
His soul had come alive, and was growing day by day.
For gradually the rose, to him, had become a symbol of forgiveness and promise
And hope; and with his life now, he was becoming more able to cope.

No longer did he look unkept, no longer did he seem inept,
And there was a definite look of purpose in his every step.
For he, too, was living and growing in every way; just like the single rose
He had watered with his tears, when he had placed it on
His mother's grave, that long, ago day.

BABY BOY LOST

She sits in her rocking chair, just rocking to and fro,
For all her waking hours, day after day.
Once in a while she may whisper,
"They have taken my baby boy away."
They were on their way, to his very first day
At school, they had both so looked forward to.
When a speeding automobile, driven by a drunken
Driver rounded a street corner, and crashed
Broad side into their mini-van.

The rest she doesn't quite remember, except she
Knows her baby boy is gone.
Her mother's heart is breaking, as she keeps
On rocking as time goes on,
And she sometimes murmers to herself, I love him so,
I love him so, where, oh where, has my baby gone.

Someone places in her arms, a little boy doll
And she holds it closely to her breast.
She may pick it up, now and then and kiss its pink little cheek.
She holds him close again and begins in a singsong rhythmic monotone to speak.

*Humpty, Dumpty sat on a wall, Humpty Dumpty
Had a great fall, all the kings horses, and all the kings men;
Suddenly she stops and a look of terror crosses her ashen face
And she begins to cry, clutching the little boy doll closer to her heart.*

*Though it all happened years ago, for her, the world stopped that day.
When fate and a drunken driver took her baby boy away.
And so she rocks day after day her life slowly wasting away.
They say she will always be the same, and will know no peace or joy,
Until the day she goes home at last, to be with her baby boy.*

GOD IS

Are there days you feel so alone, when your heart
Is so heavy, it feels just like stone.
Cold, uneasy and burdened, you just can't seem to go on.
There's no one to turn to, no relief anywhere; and you ask yourself;
Where, oh, where has God gone, and left me in such utter despair.

God is, always was, always will be, even until and beyond eternity.
He is our guiding light, our mentor, our only real security.
Our pillar of strength to lean on, when we desperately need a friend.
Never will He forsake us, and on His promises we can forever depend.

When life's chilling winds of reality on us descend.
He is there with the warm blanket of assurance and hope.
He places around our weary shoulders, that with
The caprices of life, we then, may be able to cope.
When we can no longer walk; He will carry us in His
Strong and loving arms until we are once more
Able to walk on our own, and we need never, ever to feel all alone.

There may be times our life's journey becomes such a maze.
We know not the way we should turn,
the valleys so dark and lonely, and the hills so rugged and steep.
He will say, " Follow me and be not afraid, for I am with you always,
And my watch over you I will keep, for all of your days".

His is the power to lift our spirit when we are sad;
The voice that whispers deep down inside us,
"Things will be better, just wait and see, happier days are coming,
And sunshine is on its way.
Only trust, be patient and believe, tomorrow will be a brighter day."

He is the music, the sweet, sweet music of contentment we feel deep down in
Our hearts: when we have survived life's many sharp arrows and darts.
He is always there to protect and heal us, with His divine love.
He showers down upon us from His heaven above.

So ask not where God has gone, it is not He who has abandoned us:
But we, who have wandered so far from Him, we no longer hear His voice.
Reach out for His hand, he is always near by.
For He is our heavenly Father, ever calling out to us,
"Oh, my little ones, come unto me, from out in the cold.
That you may know the warmth, and the joy of my peace, and my eternal love."

LIFE CAN BE BEAUTIFUL

Life can be such a beautiful thing, be we prince or pauper, or king.
We each see the same glorious moon above, the same galaxy of stars.
The same warming sun that shines upon us from afar.
We each have a mind, a heart, and a soul.
The same Maker above, who has our life in His control.
It's just how we live and feel about life that
Makes us who we really are.

We can be born a prince and still a pauper be.
Or have been born a pauper and the riches and
glory of life be able to see.
Envy not the king who sits on his throne, for we
each have a little throne all of our own.
Family and friends and those who love us
just for who and what we are.

So let our hearts be joyful, let them be thankful too.
That God has given us the gift of life, that we alone can choose,
To be happy or sad in good times or bad.
We can say of our life, " our cup is half empty, or our cup is half full".

*If we learn to count our blessings and put our
Disappointments behind us; we will survive.
And at the end of each day, be able to say,
"It's great, so great to be alive".*

*So weep not over yesterday, and what it might have been,
but be thankful for today whatever it may bring.
And pray that for us, tomorrow, another bright
new beautiful day of our life will begin.*

FROM MY KITCHEN WINDOW

So much of God's wondrous world from my kitchen window I can see.
Each seasons' beauty, different and special in its own way.
Changing, ever changing, day by day.
In the spring, trees budding and flowering create a fairyland view.
And the grass is so fresh, so green, so new.
Song birds darting high and low, busily building their nests.
And saucy robins, the harbingers of spring,
strutting about, showing off their bright red vests.

Summer, with her varied profusion of flowers,
A rainbow of color reveals.
And acres and acres of golden grain wave quietly in the nearby fields.
Farmers, mowing, reaping, and baling tons of precious crops.
From dawn to dusk, their hard work never stops.
The hot summer days, a thunderstorm or two may bring.
Giving refreshing relief from the heat and humidity's oppressive sting.

In the fall, leaves of every color, from the picturesque trees flutter down.
And farmers, ever in the fields, are busily planting their fall crops of grain;
Hoping to finish before a killing frost comes around.
And then, almost over night, once again;
Winter has lain her snow white blanket upon the frozen ground.

My Poetic Reflections on Life

Each new day presents a different view, for rare is the day, I see nothing new.
In the morning, a beautiful sunrise, giving promise of a wonderful day.
As nature's creatures begin their daily routine of busy work and play.
A cardinal perches on my forsythia and a red-headed woodpecker,
High in the old maple tree, is busily tapping away.
And scores of purple finch swooping to and fro
unaware they are putting on a miniature air show.

Out on the county road a school bus, looking like a small yellow box.
Picks up tiny little people on their way to school.
Then slowly, slowly moves out of sight, and I say a little prayer,
May they all return home safely tonight.

Black and white cattle on a hillside, quietly grazing away in the lush green fields.
Occasionally a deer or two, venture out from the
Nearby woods, and a furtive mouthful steals.
Up in the air, vapor trails, criss-cross the cloudless sky.
And I wonder who might the passengers be and
Where are they bound, as they slowly, slowly,
Disappear from sight, without a sound.

Water towers, like huge mushrooms, catch my eye, here and there
On the outskirts of a small town nearby.
And feathery plumes of smoke from pencil-like

Smokestacks miles and miles away.
Speak of their bustling activity each and every day.
The faraway mountains create a magnificent backdrop for this beautiful view.
Becoming a lovely scalloped curtain appropriate for any scene or any time.
Surrounding this huge open air theater of mine.

Old Mister Sun begins to set and he takes his final bow.
As he discreetly slips behind a fluffy pink and purple cloud.
Darkness approaches slowly and peace and quiet seem to settle all around.
The lights of the city begin to come into view and I can
Imagine tired folks hurrying home, when their long day's work is through.
Right on time the moon begins to rise and myriad stars start
To twinkle in the darkened skies.

Tis such a panoramic view from my kitchen window I can see.
Always there, in spring, summer, winter, or fall.
It matters not if it's snowing or raining or sunshine is over all.
The show goes on, whether in twilight or morning dew.
Perfectly directed, perfectly timed and the actors always on cue.
From my private box, I feel as privileged as a queen.
Watching a show more exciting than any from stage or screen.
Life's many little dramas as they unfold right before my eyes.
Ever old, ever new, as the days, the seasons, and the years go by.

TELL SOMEONE YOU LOVE THEM

There's nothing like a loving word to lift a heavy heart.
There's nothing like hearing from an old friend when you are miles and miles apart.
Real friendships never really die, they just kind of fade away, as time goes by.
So tell someone, today, you love them, if you really, really do.
They'll be so glad to hear those words, especially when they come from you.
Don't wait for some very special time, for that day may never come.
Try to remember just how long it's been, since they were last heard from.

They might be a family member, a long ago friend,
or even a childhood buddy you once knew.
They might even now be lonely, and sad, and thinking about you too.
It would be so great to tell them in person, but a note, or chat on the phone might do.
The words need not be flowery, only very sincere and true.
But they'll lift the heart of that someone, you long, so long ago knew.
Just let them know they are remembered, for the happy times you have shared.

And though time and space have kept you far apart;
They have never been forgotten, and you will always keep them in your heart.

Life is so uncertain and we never know when, or if, we will see them again.
Don't wait for the day, they have passed away.
For then, they can no longer hear, the kind words you may have wanted to say.
You may shed bitter tears of remorse and regret, for you never
took the time to tell them, though far apart, you still thought of them yet.
We live such busy lives, the days and years pass so quickly away.
So tell someone today you love them, you'll be ever so glad if you do;
For it will make that special someone so very happy.
And you will be happy, oh, so happy too.

TWILIGHT LOVE

They met in a nursing home, neither had ever been wed.
Both were in their eighties, or so it had been said.
They would place their chairs together, near enough to chat,
As they recalled the days they had been so young and fair.
Neither had found the right one, with whom their life to share.
They spoke of life and living and the children they never had;
And they were so happy to have met, for there
Had been times they were quite lonely and sad.

One day I saw him reach tentatively for her hand.
And in a trembling voice I heard him say,
"Oh, but could we have met many years ago,
When you were twenty one and I was twenty two.
Our lives could have been so very different, I
Really think they would have been, don't you".
Always gallant , he now and then pushes
Her wheelchair up and down the hall.
Proud as a prince with his lovely lady, walking
So very carefully so that he doesn't fall.

I brush away a tear that comes suddenly to my eye,
Thinking of the beautiful years together they
Might have had;
If they had but met those precious lost years ago,
And to each other had been wed.

Love is like a soothing balm, no matter what the age.
Someone to talk to, someone to understand.
Someone you know cares about you,
And once in a while just holds your hand.
It may be a fleeting moment, but it pushes back the years.
And it makes the heart feel younger,
Sometimes may even bring on a tear.
Just to have a real friendship you cherish,
With someone you know is sincere.

And I think again of that sweet old pair and
Send to heaven a little prayer,
That in their remaining years, some joy and
Happiness together they may share.

YESTERDAY

Take me back to yesterday, oh, how I wish you could.
When life was more relaxed, and people thought their life was good.
Working hard, yet enjoying life, in their own quiet way.
As they went about their labors each and every day.

Children respected their elders, and were taught to say " Yes Ma'am and Yes Sir".
Just as their parents and grandparents before them were.
Parents assisted them with their homework to make sure their grades were good.
And kept a close eye on them, all through, and even after childhood..
Morning chores over, they hastened off to school, and when the school bell rang,
Saying classes were through; hurried back home again, their evening chores to do.

Saturday night was bath night and each one took his turn.
And a goodly supply of warm water was their major concern.
Mother laid out their very best clothes for Sunday morning church.
Making sure the boys had a nice clean white shirt, and the girls were prettily dressed.
And that all their garments had been very carefully pressed.

Next morning chores done, we all climbed into our twenty-nine Chevy.
Not too long ago, we would have ridden in our old horse-drawn buggy.
At church, we knew we must listen to the preacher and once in a while, with him say, Amen.
And sing the beautiful old hymns that still go through my mind, now and again.

Church over, someone might ask us to their house for dinner.
Or we invited someone to ours.
If it happened to be the preacher and his wife
The meal might just go on for hours.
Daddy would say grace and we could hardly wait.
The company was always served first, before
We got anything on our plate.

There was oyster stew and tiny little crackers if we wanted to be fancy.
Sometimes a bowl of cole-slaw from our very favorite Aunt Nancy.
Always fried chicken a plenty, but we still held our breath.
Afraid the grownups might be so hungry they might not leave us any.
Country ham from our own smoke house.
Mama wanted it special today, for sister was here with her brand-new spouse.
Sweet corn, and lima beans, and tomatoes fresh from the vine.
Fresh lemonade and ice tea, a generous piece of chocolate cake, me, oh my,
Or Grandma's fresh homemade apple pie.

Oh, it was a generous repast, it seemed each family
Would try to outdo the other.
The wonderful Sunday dinners we had.
The children gulped down their food and asked to be excused,

That they might go outside and play hopscotch, jump rope,
Or hide and seek, the favorites of the day.
The older boys played ball, keeping a sharp ear out
For the time to go home, when their father would give them a call.

The men sat around discussing the local news and if the weather was good,
They had themselves a good old time outside, pitching horseshoes,
Oh, they hadn't played the game since they couldn't remember when.
And, they'd better get in some practice or Grandpa'd beat them all over again.

The ladies cleared the dishes, chatted about the weather, and exchanged a recipe or two.
Someone might drop a secret about a tiny little arrival she was expecting come the fall.
And there would be oohs and ahs and congratulations from them all.
Late afternoon, they all went home their evening chores to do.
We chatted then amongst ourselves what a nice day it had been for us too.
How we hoped we could do it again soon and
The next time maybe we could have some good beef stew.
When night came, Mama hurried us upstairs to bed;
Carrying the coal oil lamp on ahead, "No, we couldn't carry it", she said.

We knelt on our knees, and thanked the Lord for
His blessings and the wonderful day it had been.

And let us wake in the morning, Lord, if you would,
And please forgive our sin.
Oh, if I could only go back there again, just for a little while.
To see for sure how it all had been, and that I hadn't dreamed it after all;
And my old mind wasn't playing tricks on me again.
For it had been so lovely, the life we lived back then.
There seemed to have been more laughter and
More love and concern shared with family and friends.

I guess they call it progress, I guess they call it success.
For me, I'd just as soon do it that way again, but I guess
Folks would say I had regressed.
Oh, I tell my great grandchildren how great it was back then.
But they don't seem to be so very impressed.

We had our quiet times, we had our times of fun.
We took the time to worship, and could peacefully rest, when our day's work was done.
So thank you Lord, for the times that have been and I believe in your Heaven above,
The joy, the peace, the quiet, the love, and more I will live all over again.

HE THOUGHT HER BONNY

Oh, but he thought her bonny.
Oh, but he thought her fair.
Her blue eyes ever dancing.
The sunlight on her golden hair.

Did he know she thought him handsome.
Did he know she thought him strong.
Did he know she dreamed about him.
Did he know, in her heart, he was her song.

Came the day, he tried to say, in his own shy way;
That he loved her only, and hoped they would someday wed.
She touched his lips, with her fingertips,
As though words need not be said;
For she already knew, and she had wanted that, too.
A new chapter in their lives had now just begun.
For their two young hearts were now beating as one.

Together now, they walk hand in hand.
Each wearing the other's golden band.
With them, two little girls with golden hair, and dancing eyes of blue.
And two little boys most handsome , two little boys so strong.
Looking just like their daddy, as they happily tag along.
A more beautiful family picture I have rarely ever seen.
So young, so loving, so happy, so serene,
and part of many a young heart's wistful dream.

FOREVER TOGETHER

She sat by his side, watching his life slowly ebb away.
Sixty-odd years together they had, had.
She smiled as she recalled their wedding day,
So many precious memories seemed to pass before her eyes.
They had climbed life's mountains together
And played in life's sunny warm sand.
They had laughed and cried together, and through the storms
Of life, they had held each others' hand.
Three children had been born to them,
And grandchildren, and great-grandchildren had blessed them.
And one little great-great-grandson, who looked so much like him.
She reached to touch his cheek and for a fleeting moment,
He looked at her, then said, " I love you".
And she whispered softly, "I love you, too".
Then came from his lips a little sigh as though he was saying good bye,
And she knew he had passed on, and that from this earth he had gone.
Tearfully, she reached her hand toward him and in a whisper said,
"Would that I could be with you".
God, above, must have heard her prayerful plea.
For in that moment, she, too, had passed on.
To be with him in eternity.
I think of that dear old couple, so special and in this world so blessed.
And pray that in eternity they will now, forever together, peacefully rest.

MESSAGE OF SPRING

Spring, spring, ah, beautiful spring.
The most wondrous time of the year.
Daffodils, tulips, and crocus over night appear.
Song birds, busily building their nests,
Right on time, at nature's behest.
Suddenly, all the earth seems to awake,
From winter's cold night, to spring's daybreak.
Flowering shrubs and trees delight the eye.
The warming sun in an azure blue sky.
Easter's glorious message of renewal and hope.
A sacrifice made for us, beyond our mental scope.
When, Jesus, our savior, died on that cruel cross,
To atone for our sins, that our souls be not lost.
From the tomb he arose, on that Easter Morn.
And the hope of heaven, to mankind was born.
May we store the essence of spring, deep in our soul,
To sustain us, when life becomes listless and cold.
What a comfort for us, that could be,
For the joy, the beauty, and the glory of life, we then will see.
So, thank you Lord, for the blessings and beauty of spring,
And for the message of hope and renewal,
Of our spirit it will bring.
And may we then, like the songbirds, in spring,
Your praises, forever joyfully sing.

MY VISION

I had been severely ill that day, so weak, so weary, I could scarcely lift my head.
Languishing there with complications following surgery.
When I saw Him standing at the foot of my bed.
The magnificence of His presence seemed to fill the room,
And there was an aura of light around Him, that dispelled away all gloom.
Was He real, or was I dreaming, the great sense of peace, I was feeling.
He was clothed in a long purple robe and there was a golden sash around
His waist, and with a mass of golden curls, His handsome head was graced.
His countenance was that of an angel with a loving caring smile, so serene,
Unlike any other I have ever seen.

He stood there looking down on me in such an inquisitive way.
As though He was wondering if He should
Take me with him, or if He should let me stay.
Then for a moment He seemed to back away;
Only to move forward again, as though He was going to speak.
But then, He just smiled down on me in that same caring way.
Then slowly, slowly, silently moved backward and
My beautiful vision had faded away.

Had He reached out and taken my hand and bade me go with him.
I would have gone willingly and joyfully, and never looked back or shed a tear.
So beautiful, so unspeakably caring He had been.
The glorious ethereal presence that had appeared at the foot of my bed.
I know, some day, He will come again and I will have no fear.
Only peace and bliss and unspeakably joy, when he comes again,
This time, to take me home with Him.

LAMENT

The other day I heard a man say, in a kind of sad lament,
His whole life in mediocrity had been spent.
While a friend he knew, really had it all.
He was handsome, he was brilliant, all who knew him, loved him.
And he must have had his very own mint,
The luxurious life he lived, and the reams of money he spent.
He went on further to say if he could be exactly like his friend,
He would be so very content and his enjoyment of life would never end.

I began to think to myself, if we were all exactly alike,
What a dull old world this would be.
If no one seemed to be inferior, no one could feel superior.
If there were no one poorer, there could be no one richer.
If everyone was a king, who would his subjects be.
If there were only teachers, who would be their students and who would pay their fee.
If there were only those who wrote the music, who would sing their songs.
If everyone just planted the fields, who would there be to reap the yields.
If everyone looked exactly alike, who would there be to admire.
And, then where would there be, even for a moment anyone we might desire.

We stand not alone in this world, and on one another we sorely depend.
In God's master plan, we each compliment or enhance the lives of one another.
For our lives are intertwined as closely as if everyone was our brother.
We interact with one another, whether in relationships of love, or work, or play.
There will always be someone to give us courage, or someone who may take it away.
Before we can become a giver there has to be a receiver.
Before we can ever make our point there has to be a believer.
There has to be a buyer before there can be a seller.
Before we can draw our money from the bank there needs to be a teller.
One can't even play catch unless there's someone to throw the ball.
And it could never be said we won the race if there was no one there to make the call.

So let's not complain, born we handsome or born we plain.
God really didn't have to make us at all.
It's our diversity that makes this old world go around.
Some fly high, up in the sky, some are happier on the ground.
God loves us all alike, He loves no one less.

He loves none of us more;
Whether He allows us to be rich, or allows some of us to be poor.
I believe for each of us He opens a special door.

For He has a very special niche, that only
We can fill in our own unique way.
As we go about our individual lives day after day.

Having done our very best, let us not envy the rest,
But try to accept the place in life we find ourselves to be.
As for the place and time in which God has placed me,
I feel more than content.

Though I have few attributes of which I can proudly boast
And of this world's treasures I haven't had the most.
I am content, just being who I am, and where I am.
And I can say with conviction and I say it not to be bold,
Contentment brings it's own riches, more precious than silver or gold.
For it gives one a sense of peace and well being deep in our soul.

This, then, will my life's motto be, and if you would
like to join me, please, repeat after me —
As for me, I will strive to be, the very best me
I know I can be, and as content in life as I choose to be.

THE MARATHON OF LIFE

Life is like a marathon, a race of endurance that will test even the fit and strong.
Not to be taken lightly, for the course for us may be rough and long.
Once we enter the race, there can be no dropping out,
And mile after mile, we discover what life's great marathon is all about.
One never knows if they will finish first, or last, or somewhere in between.
The most important thing is to run by the rules, and to run the long race clean.

Some in the race may be sprinters, who run the race like a hundred-yard dash.
Pushing and shoving others out of their way; showing no deference
To anyone who might by chance, into their path stray.
Some may be plodders, slow of foot, yet strong of heart.
Struggling, always struggling, from the very start, yet still they
Manage somehow to finish the race, against all odds, and finish with dignity and grace.

Many must run against the strong winds of adversity and some in the pouring rain.
Some may run with vim and vigor, and some may run with pain.
There are those who might stop to assist a
fellow traveler, who may have fallen by the way.
That he may regain his footing and run again another day.

My Poetic Reflections on Life

There may be someone, just jogging along, who seeing
A field of beautiful wild flowers that take his breath away,
May slow down for just a moment, the glorious sight to survey.
Some may reach a time in their life, they believe they can no longer go on.
But, then, something deep inside their soul gives them courage and
Determination enough to put those running shoes back on.

There are some, who, when they cross the finish line, fall numbly to the ground.
Exhausted, remembering nothing of beauty or satisfaction,
And in the long, long race, nothing of joy have they found.
And then there are those who have finished far behind the rest,
But have wonderful memories of their life experiences
And they feel so very specially blessed.
For they ran their race with valor and honor and always did their best.
Victory can be sweet, finish where we may, but it will be even sweeter,
If we stopped for just a moment or two and smelled the lovely
Flowers we saw along our way.

LITTLE ONE LOST

My little one, my little one.
Your Dad and I so looked forward to.
We loved you from the very start.
But then one day, you went away,
And returned to God from whom you came.
Heaven can only be more beautiful.
For your sweet presence there,
And we will know you're forever safe,
Within God's tender care.
And though for only a fleeting moment
You filled our lives with joy and love,
and then we had to part;
My love for you, my little one.
Will now, forever be, cradled within my heart.

Printed in the United States
142983LV00006B/30/A